THE 50
SECRETS OF HIGHLY
SUCCESSFUL
CATS

THE 50 SECRETS OF HIGHLY SUCCESSFUL CATS

COLLEEN Q. O'SHEA
AND
CRUMBUM Q. MCINTOSH

Illustrated by Mike Flint

A Dell Trade Paperback

A DELL TRADE PAPERBACK

Published by
Dell Publishing
a division of
Bantam Doubleday Dell Publishing Group, Inc.
1540 Broadway
New York, New York 10036

Copyright © 1994 by Catherine L. O'Shea and
Michael J. O'Shea
Illustrations copyright © 1994 by Mike Flint
Book design by Susan Maksuta

The trademark Dell® is registered in the U.S.
Patent and Trademark Office.

Library of Congress Cataloging in Publication Data

O'Shea, Colleen Q.
        The 50 secrets of highly successful cats /
    Colleen Q. O'Shea and Crumbum Q. McIntosh :
    illustrated by Mike Flint.
            p. cm.
        ISBN 0-440-50635-2
        1. Cats—Humor. I. McIntosh; Crumbum Q.
II. Title.
    PN6231.C23O74   1994
    818′.5402—dc20   94-4216
                                                CIP

Printed in the United States of America

Published simultaneously in Canada

December 1994

10 9 8 7 6 5 4 3 2 1

FFG

For Gloria, the Musical Cat,
and her dear friend, Jane

FOREPAUSE:
An authors' introduction

Love being a cat? Of course you do. Cats are uniquely gifted. Who else can keep a house vermin free, serve as the office paperweight (while answering the phone), *and* warm the bed at night?

Cats are adaptable and self-reliant enough to live successfully in almost any environment: alone, with other cats—we've even heard of cats who effectively supervise goats, horses, and d-o-g-s.

The inescapable fact, however, is that our lives are richest when we share them with caring, well-trained humans. Who else will feed us *virtually* on demand; play games of *our* choosing; provide laps, comfort, and treats; and (frequently) refrain from laughing at us when we (occasionally) miscalculate?

Now, we know the standard wisdom as well as you do. Who hasn't groaned over that old tail twitcher, "Why do cats have nine lives?

. . . Because they spend eight of them training their humans!"

Respectfully, we beg to differ. We've trained our well-meaning but average humans, without *that* much effort, to be delightful companions. Our secret? We stopped focusing on their limited skills—they'll never be able to curl up in the mixing bowl—and honed our own skills as cats. *Our* expertise has prompted them to stretch their own horizons in response.

This book, then, focuses on *cat* behavior in the cat/human household. In a convenient, alphabetical listing you'll find everything you need to know (from the appropriate use of outside-the-box "accidents" to strategies for getting the treats *you* want) to maximize your opportunities for living the good life and minimize the frustrations of dealing, daily, with humans' limited abilities and comprehension.

Using this book, you'll be able to establish a rewarding cat-human relationship at your

house and still have time—in this lifetime—
for a nap!

    Colleen Q. O'Shea
    Crumbum Q. McIntosh

P.S. If, after reading our rules and practicing
them consistently for a month, you still have
questions, feel free to write us at "Colleen &
Mac," P.O. Box 1203, Newberry, S.C., 29108.
There is no additional charge for a follow-up
catsultation.

THE 50
SECRETS OF HIGHLY
SUCCESSFUL
CATS

1. "Accidents," strategic use of

(If you have questions on basic litter skills, see your mother. Our concern lies, literally, *outside* the litter box.)

Two kinds of "accidents" are in every skilled cat's repertoire:

a. "The Reminder Accident": Always place this *near* a poorly maintained litter box. After a couple of these, your humans will rush to keep your box fresh and inviting.

b. "The Political/Philosophical Accident": Sometimes (say, when your humans have been on vacation, ignored you, brought a strange child into your home, or said "no" once too often) a cat simply has to make a statement. In these extreme cases, we recommend the "P/P Accident," preferably: (1) in a corner, (2) in a running shoe, or (3) on the *TV Guide.*

Remember: "Accidents" are potent training tools. Use them wisely.

See also: *Attention*
            Training

2. Antiques, helping your humans acquire

As a sensitive household manager, you should always be mindful of your humans' special interests. If these include indoor sports and cooking, count yourself lucky. With a little effort, however, you can demonstrate your enthusiasm for other human pursuits as well. Antiques are a case in point.

An "antique" is something (or someone) humans bring into the house so they can stand around, look at it, and admire it a lot. When it's furniture, they often take it apart, pour something nasty over it, rub it, and otherwise play with it for days on end. Truly interesting antiques have bumps, nicks, marks, and scratches. Which is, of course, where you can help considerably.

If it's made of cloth, you can wrinkle, soak, soil, or shred it; if it's wood, you can nick it or scratch it; if it's ceramic, one good shove can often provide both chips and cracks. Just use the special seventh sense all cats have concerning good antiques, and you'll select the right "help" for each product. After you've offered only one such treatment, your family will lavish attention on you if you so much as look at the item with interest again.

3. Attention, eight infallible ways to get humans'

A senior housecat is often too busy to need much human attention. From time to time, however, even the most self-sufficient cat can profit from a little human-feline interaction. At those moments, try some of these carefully tested attention-getting maneuvers. We've keyed these examples to accommodate various levels of catspertise.

If your target human is standing:

a. (Basic): Wrap around his ankles.

b. (Intermediate): Climb his legs far enough to tap on (or nip) his kneecap.

c. (Advanced): Climb the highest piece of furniture in his line of vision (preferably one with antiques on it) and do vigorous calisthenics, while moaning loudly.

d. (Infallible, but crude): Pee on his shoes.

If your target human is sitting, working:

a. (Basic): Sit facing her, staring intently. (Important: Do NOT blink.)

b. (Intermediate): Sit *on* whatever she's working with/on.

c. (Advanced): Liberate her pencil, marker, scissors, or what-have-you. (Modification for computers: Stomp on the keyboard.)

d. (Infallible, but crude): Throw a fur ball on her completed work.

See also: *"Accidents"*
            Eye Contact

4. Basic Vocabulary (to ignore): For instance, "Heere, kitty"; "No"

Humans periodically get "upset." (Their reasons for this will almost certainly be incomprehensible; don't worry about them.) Upset humans can aggravate their condition by repeating certain phrases. These include (but are not limited to) "Heere, kitty, kitty, kitty," "No. I said no!" "Stop that. Now!" and "Get off."

Since you're there to lessen human suffering, your responsibility is clear: The experienced cat *never* responds to these phrases. Doing so would only encourage their use and extend your humans' distress. So take the high road. When you hear these (or similar) phrases, disappear, bite, or go selectively deaf.

See also: *Biting*
Evasion
Eye Contact
Hiding

5. Beds, ten best bets for

The world's best beds meet at least three of these criteria:

a. They were not originally designed to be cat beds.

b. They were not provided for your sleeping pleasure.

c. You discovered/created/appropriated them yourself.

d. You can share them with someone you love.

When shopping for a bed you must, therefore, rigorously avoid any bed purchased or built just for you. Instead, seek places that are soft; warm; a good "fit" for you; quiet, but not too removed from family activities; and—most important—uniquely possessing the quality of "my bedness." (You alone will recognize this attribute.) In our experience, potentially great bed locations include:

a. Under the sink, if grocery bags live there.

b. On top of the oven or dryer, while in use.

c. In a mixing bowl, in a warm kitchen cupboard.

d. In the linen closet, for obvious reasons.

e. In a half-open dresser drawer.

f. Over an in-floor heat vent.

g. On a closet shelf, especially one with woolen hats, scarves, and the like.

h. In an office in/out basket, especially when full; or a laundry basket, ditto.

i. Behind the books on the lower shelf of a large bookcase (particularly good for the extra naps required when small children are in the house).

j. In/on any bed, sofa, or chair shared with your favorite sleeping human.

See also: *Hiding*
             Location
             Placeology

6. Biting (the hand that feeds you, pets you, etc.)

Why is this even an issue?

Simply put, most humans hate biting. They see it as an *attack*, rather than the effective "short-paw" communication it is. For instance, when you're tired of being petted you could run away, vocalize "please stop now," or contort yourself uncomfortably to avoid the stroking hand. Or you could quickly end the session with a well-placed bite.

Humor your humans whenever you can. But when biting seems called for,* be incisive. Don't debate: Bite.

------

* For other instances where biting may be required, see also *Carriers, Collars,* and *Vets.*

7. Blame, sharing the

As an experienced, busy cat, you will usually ignore humans' negative reactions to anything you choose to do. (Any response from you merely encourages their inappropriate behaviors.) On occasion, however, the negative force of their reaction, if directed unequivocally at you, might damage the delicate balance of your relationship. In such cases, if you live in a multipet household, or one containing small children, remain calm. By acting promptly and subtly, you usually can create enough human doubt concerning who did what to avoid direct personal punishment.

For instance, if you've left something nasty (a wet spot, a fur ball, yesterday's dinner) where it should not be, you may:

a. Stick close to your humans until they discover your achievement.

b. Outdo them in surprise: Stop short and

jump back in horror, fluffing your fur while you turn to them loudly lamenting this startling development. (This ruse works for us every time.)

See also: *Basic Vocabulary (to ignore)*
            Cleaning
            Hiding

8. Carriers

Carriers are bad news. They lead to flea dips, vacation trips, or (perish the thought) vets. Despite their cute names (Kitty Caddy, PortaPet, Taxi Cat), carriers take us where we don't want to go, when we don't want to go there. Carriers must—and can—be stopped.

Our first carrier was cardboard and easily dealt with: We ate it. Although the new models are plastic and metal, you can escape these too. Remember, no carrier can take you away if you're not in it. Practice *avoidance*.

How?

First, any cat can hear, at any distance, the soft *thud/clink* of a quietly opened carrier. (With practice, you can even hear your humans *thinking* about opening the carrier.) When you hear carrier noises, move fast: Disappear.

If this fails, demonstrate your ability to

defy the superstitions humans call the laws of physics.* Try:

a. "The expanding universe": Swell up to eight times your normal size.

b. "The four-squared hypotenuse": Extend and lock all four legs to exceed the area of the carrier door. (Also called the "spread-eagle" defense.)

c. "The dead-weight drop": When you're being stuffed in, suddenly shift your body weight to the part of you that your humans are *not* holding. You'll be free and on your feet in no time flat.

---

* If physics prevails, see also: *"Accidents"*
                                                      Biting
                                                      Evasion
                                                     Exercises
                                                     Hiding

9. Cat's Meow, and your broader vocabulary

Humans, even the best of them, seem to believe that cats say only "meow."* We almost *never* say that. (We once heard a kitten say "meow," but it was a slip of the tongue.)

In fact, the longer you live with humans, the more you will refine your vocabulary, using words guaranteed to get the best results. For instance, we—or friends of ours—have successfully used these words in cat-to-human conversations:

Say:	*To indicate:*
Grrr . . .	Anger/warning
Irk; Now?	Helpfulness/alertness
Me?	Cuteness/expectation
Murph?	Curiosity/interest

Nothing (See "Moon")	Indignation
Ow! Raoul!	Pain/terror
Prrr . . .	Pleasure/joy
Whee!	Playfulness
Wow! Hey!	Amazement
Zzzz . . .	Restfulness

You probably know others. If not, listen, learn, and have fun!

---

* To be fair, some humans have better hearing. In *Ulysses*, for example, James Joyce's cats say things like "mkgnao" and "mrkgnao" (appropriate for an Irish cat), while Kurt Vonnegut's cats use appropriate American idioms like "Ralph."

10. Cat Toys

Well-meaning humans always misunderstand this term. They think it means balls, bells, squeaky rubber creatures, or, sadly, even complex contraptions like one recently advertised as follows: "Watch your cat play for hours with the nonstop rolling ball chase!"

The sophisticated cat will never play with such so-called toys. If you're feeling exceptionally gracious you may, however, help your *humans* enjoy them, after all their trouble. You might, therefore, paw a store-bought toy once or twice— just to exercise your humans—before you sit on it or swat it under the sofa. *Real* cat toys

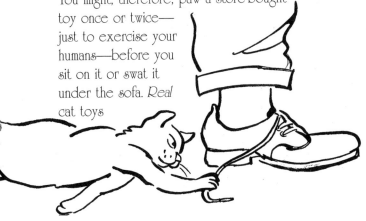

include jewelry, coins, pens,* pencils,* telephones, toupees,* paper clips,† shoe laces,† twist ties,† and important documents.†

---

*For maximum enjoyment (both yours and your humans'), play with these *while* your humans are using them. Fun for the entire family!

†These items are frequently "food" as well. See *Food and Unfood* and *Games*.

11. Cause and Effect, human fallacies regarding

We hate to disillusion you, but facts are facts: Humans simply don't understand cause and effect. True, they can quote the First Law of the Cat Universe quite correctly in Latin. (*Post hoc, ergo propter hoc*, or "After this, therefore because of this.") Unfortunately, humans regard it as a fallacy!

Cats, on the other hand, clearly understand simple causal relationships. Here's a good example: Recently everyone at our house was watching an interesting picture in the picture window. Our humans called it "torrential downpour." Trying to look more closely, we accidentally touched the window with our nose. Immediately the picture changed to "bolt of lightning hits neighbor's tree." It was terrifying, so we never touched the window with our nose again. In fact, we now nap under the bed when the torrential-downpour picture is in the window. By refusing to activate the bolt-of-lightning picture again, we know we've saved many neighborhood trees.

If you share such moments with your humans, you may finally help them understand. *You* know the day begins when you wake up. Someday your humans will see this truth too.

See also: *Placeology*
  Televisions, Washing Machines, and Windows

12. Cleaning (as a "political" statement)

(Note: This entry is not about hygiene. We assume you've mastered the basics of personal cleanliness. Special note to long-hairs: Don't waste your time. Simply leave your grooming to somebody else.)

The successful cat has refined cleaning to a high art. By choosing the proper time, place, and attitude (that is, whether you face those sharing space with you or not), you can use cleaning as:

- A carefully calculated *snub:* Washing with your back to someone is more assertive than refusing to make eye contact but more gracious than a "full moon."

- A *stall:* Unsure of your next step in a delicate negotiation? Wash while you think it over.

- A *cover,* to avoid potential embarrassment: Did the unthinkable happen? Did you, for instance, actually miscalculate a jump and slide off the top of the TV? When you hit the floor, casually placing your back leg over your head to wash your hindquarters can become an integral part of your Screw-up Recovery Program.

See also: *Eye Contact*
            Moon
            Recovery After Errors

13. Collars, escaping from

Has this happened to you? You're sitting around minding your own business, when suddenly a human grabs you and, without apology, ties a collar around your neck. Nobody knows why. You should be able to avoid having the collar placed on you, but what should you do if you fail? There's still a chance to escape the collar. The answer is simple and straightforward:

a. Run around the house as fast as you can.

b. After your run, rest, occasionally moving very suddenly (in the hope of catching the collar off guard).

c. Looking very devious, skulk backward around the entire house (in the hope that the change of direction confuses the collar into falling off).

We can't lie to you: These steps failed the last time we tried them. But we remain convinced of their effectiveness, and we'll use them again if need be.

See also: *Biting*
             Evasion
             Exercises

14. Cute, Being: A fairly effective persuader

Need quick human approval? Some say being cute (playful, friendly, cuddly) always works.

The key to successful cuteness is to calibrate your behavior to the importance of the desired result. For instance, asking your humans to open a door (unless your litter box is behind it) never merits the same effort as asking for food. The following scale should help:

a. Minimum Cute (You just want a refresher pat.):
   Put your head under a human's hand and rub. (In our house, we call this maneuver "The Self-Patting Kitty.")

b. Moderate Cute (You want to be invited to share the bed.):
   Sit picturesquely by the side of the bed, staring soulfully into their eyes, mewing

softly. Every time they glance your way, twitch your tail and bonk your head on the edge of the bed.

c. Full-press Cute (It's dinnertime!):
Rub their legs, making little sounds of encouragement, and lead them toward the kitchen. If they show signs of becoming distracted en route, fall down, roll on your back, and invite tummy rubs. Once in the kitchen, rub against everything in sight (especially the pantry and/or refrigerator

doors), twirl around their ankles, and
continue vocal encouragement.

See also: *Dinnertime*
             "Dog" Tricks
             Eye Contact

15. Dinnertime

Dinnertime is pretty much whenever you're hungry. Don't be a slave to fashion or to human preoccupation with clocks. Assert your rights as chief household scheduler. If your stomach says it's dinnertime, get someone's attention and go for it. If you use your cuteness tricks, sequentially, on every human in the house, *someone* is bound to feed you.

See also: *Attention*
            Cute, Being
            "Expectation"
            Food and Unfood
            Food-related Noises

16. "Dog" Tricks (rolling over, begging, etc.)

Many humans find "dog" tricks appealing, especially in puppies. Does this mean cats should do such tricks too?

No.

See also: *Cute, Being*
            "Expectation"

17. Emergencies, creating, for fun and practice

Like radio stations and the Pentagon, cats must constantly be ready for any emergency. What would you do, for instance, if any of the following threatened your home:

Bad food	Humans you don't already know
Dogs	Monsters
Garbage trucks	Vacuum cleaning

The correct procedure, when faced with *any* of these disasters, is to run around the house faster than you've ever run before with your tail grotesquely inflated behind you. (This makes intruders fear you're a rabid raccoon.)

To prepare yourself for these, and other, cat-astrophes, schedule several times a week to pretend that the scariest item on your list has happened, and respond accordingly. (Don't let little obstacles like crystal lamps slow you down. Your humans love to watch them teeter precariously as you whiz by.) To make your simulation as realistic as possible, schedule it while your humans are working, sleeping, using the phone, or otherwise "indisposed." They'll be glad to see that you are always on the job.

See also: *Exercises*

18. Evasion

Experienced cats routinely use evasive tactics to avoid an unpleasant outcome. Classically referred to as the "Veni, vidi, vamoose" ("I came, I saw, I vanished") maneuver, evasion must be quick and complete. For instance, say you hear a carrier being lifted and, a few minutes later, your humans appear, all friendly and gentle. Don't be (literally) taken in. Leave the room *immediately*, zigging and zagging as needed to avoid their clutching hands. The key here is to *vanish*, asap. (**Note**: This might be a good time for a secret nap behind the books!)

See also: *Carriers*
             Exercises
             Hiding
             Placeology
             Vets

19. Exercises

Few species sleep as much as we do, or as well. Why? Because they're in bad health (and they suffer pangs of conscience, but that's another story).

Our good health results from two factors: (a) We're very selective in our diet, and (b) we get enough exercise.

For a comprehensive exercise program, combine regular emergency drills with any of the following.

Aerobatics

Leap or climb to the top of the highest furniture available and dive into a chair. (To turn this into an emergency drill, wait until the chair is occupied.)

Drapery Rappelling

Claws extended, race as quickly as you can up one drape, run across the curtain rod or valence and *back* down the other drape, paw over paw. (If you yowl loudly, you won't be annoyed by the sometimes-harsh ripping sound accompanying parts of this exercise.)

Furniture Steeplechase

When no human is present, jump from chair to chair, possibly adding a detour to the mantel, just for kicks. This exercise is especially rewarding when a human turns it into a game by trying to pick you up. In that case, run *under* a chair. Wait. When the human gets down in position to grab you, run under the next chair or table. (And so on.) You can do this indefinitely, but—for your human's sake—you should probably limit sessions to three hours each.

People Slalom

Without breaking stride, run several times (in random order) around the ankles of all the people in the room. This exercise can also be used as emergency training, especially if the people start falling down.

See also: *Emergencies*
Evasion
Food and Unfood
Games

20. "Expectation": An effective, low-stress ploy

Creating a convincing air of expectation is a remarkably simple two-step process. First, sit at full alert. (It is sometimes especially effective to twitch, tremble, or sway a little.) Second, give your humans a wide-eyed, unblinking, concentrated stare, radiating confidence, eagerness, and faith.

The intensity, innocence, and goodwill of the "expectation ploy" has, we're told, been known to deflect suspicion even when the cat had actual canary feathers on her lips. While we can't comment on that, we have used it effectively to gain six extra pieces of "candy," an opportunity to spend the night on the bed, and other "perks" too numerous to mention here.

The beauty of "expectation" is that it's less demanding and much less humiliating than a

"dog trick" and accomplishes the same result.
Try it soon!

See also: *Cute, Being*
            Dinnertime
            Eye Contact
            Treats

21. Eye Contact (with humans): When to make; when to avoid

Eye contact can be a valuable communications tool, if used judiciously. Fortunately, the rules governing its use are fairly straightforward.

Make eye contact when:

a. You want them to do something.
b. You want them to stop doing something (singing, for example; humans persist in thinking they can sing).
c. *You* start any conversation.
d. You merely wish to reassert your aura.

Refuse to make eye contact when:

a. They have initiated a boring conversation.
b. You're affecting deafness because they want you either to do something or to stop doing something.

c. However rarely, one of your plans misfires and you suspect they may be laughing at you.

d. You're giving a favorite human the "Full Treatment": Sitting on his chest purring, kneading, and swaying slightly, *with your eyes closed in bliss.*

See also: *Attention*
            Basic Vocabulary (to ignore)
            Cleaning
            "Expectation"
            Recovery After Errors

22. Food and Unfood: How to tell the difference

Food is anything you want to eat (paper clips, the centerpiece, your humans' dessert, and—at least eight times a day—fresh cat food).

Unfood is anything you *don't* want to eat, especially when it is in your dish.

When you're alone and discover something that smells tasty, be quick and be quiet. When you're fed some unfood, publicly and ceremoniously *bury* it (as you would something nasty in your litter box) under anything convenient. If nothing is handy, and trained humans are present, pantomime your reaction for at least five minutes. With any luck, they'll get the point and you'll get some food.

See also: *Rubber Bands*

23. Food-related Noises

. . . are any sounds that could mean dinnertime has arrived. Depending on how hungry you are, food-related noises may include:

- Food or water going into your dish.
- Your dish being washed.
- Your dish being picked up.
- Can opener whirring.
- Refrigerator door opening.
- Pantry door opening.
- Water running in kitchen.
- Footsteps in kitchen.
- Kitchen light going on.
- Kitchen door opening.
- Water running anywhere in house.
- Footsteps anywhere in house.
- Footsteps anywhere in neighborhood.
- Any sound you haven't heard before.
- Silence.

When you hear a FRN, find the nearest trained human and become irresistibly cute.

See also: *Cute, Being*
Dinnertime

24. Fur Balls

A good rule-of-paw when tossing fur balls: *Use the Oriental rug sparingly, perhaps for one fur ball in four.* It is also considered polite to aim (at least once a year) for the linoleum. Other good spots include on the bed, on business papers, in briefcases, in lingerie drawers, or in the middle of a party!

---

* A helpful hint: Most cats go for the center of the rug, not realizing the advanced clean-up opportunity they can create with a well-placed "fringe" ball. Try it. Your humans will talk *feelingly* of your heroic efforts to spare their rug.

25. Games: "Power playing"

In all sports, the name of the real game is "power." To excel at power playing, remember this:

a. The cat always chooses the game.
b. The cat always chooses when to play.
c. The cat always chooses where to play.
d. The cat sets the rules and changes them at her whim.

You usually can train a moderately intelligent human in the rules of power playing

very quickly. Say, for example, your human brings home a new "irresistible catnip ball with a tinkling bell" from the pet store (her first mistake), urging you to play fetch.

- First, you yawn and lie down with your back to her.

If she comes around in front of you and throws the ball, in what she hopes is your direction:

- You sit on it until she gives up and goes away.
- To drive your point home, you wait until she's peacefully asleep (3 A.M. is usually a good time) and then furiously bounce the ball off the frame of the bedroom door a couple of hundred times, making sure that the door rattles, the bell rings, and you growl horribly.

In most cases one of these sessions should be enough to insure that future games are played on your terms and that you never see the offending toy again.

See also: *Cat Toys*

26. Gifts

From time to time, your humans will bring you little gifts. (You will probably loathe them, but it's the thought that counts.) Since cats are unfailingly gracious, you will wish to return this favor.

Of all the gifts you could select, we most strongly recommend the dead rodent. On the one paw, it shows you took considerable trouble to surprise them. On the other, should they not need it right then, you're still ahead. *Bon appétit.*

See also: *Cat Toys*

27. Hair, tactical shedding of

Successful shedding is an art *and* a science. Pay attention to where you are.

Shedding on fabric the same color as your hair is wasted effort. If your coat is light, head for the navy blazer; if you're dark-

haired, go for the white sofa. If you're
multicolored, release contrasting fur. You
know how to do this; we all do.

28. Hiding: What to do when called

Hiding is, of course, your classic response when called. A truly successful cat also masters the art of hiding when her humans are trying to leave for the evening and want to do a feline head count before they go. At the least, their search for you gets their adrenaline pumping before they face the

outside world without your help. If you're really skilled, you may delay them so long they decide to stay home with you instead.

The bottom line on successful hiding is this: If *you* can't see *them*, they can't see you.

29. "Keep Your Sunny Side Up" (or "Heliotropism")

In planning your schedule, remember the Cats' Prime Directive: *Sequere solis* ("Follow the sun"). Only an inattentive cat sleeps needlessly in the shade. Should your humans put you through the torture of relocation, immediately mind-map the new facility, tracking the sunlight through the rooms. (A helpful hint: To find the sunniest window, watch where your humans put their plants. Chances are, that's your spot.)

See also: *Making the Rounds*

30. Location (is everything)

One occasionally sees a young kitten
following her human around, hoping for
attention. How cute, but how sad: There is
no reason to waste energy in this fashion.
Humans will invariably come to you if you are
smart.

All you have to do is station yourself along
their incredibly predictable paths. For
example, humans watching TV will invariably go
to the kitchen and/or the bathroom. Station
yourself in a doorway or corridor, preferably
where you can see them and (equally
important) they can see you. If you look
winsome when they pass by, they will either
pet you or feel guilty for not doing so. Either
way, you will not have wasted time, and you
certainly will not have wasted energy. You
can't be a kitten all your life.

Try this: If they don't pet you on the way

out, take their chair. (It will have been prewarmed.)

See also: *Attention*
             Cute, Being
             Petting

31. Making the Rounds: How senior cats choose their routes

Among your major daily responsibilities is a systematic check of your many official "places," making sure that:

a. Sunshine is where it's supposed to be.
b. Your windows are showing the appropriate pictures.
c. All food locations are adequately stocked.
d. The litter box is appropriately maintained.
e. Other areas of major olfactory importance (the kitchen, the basement, the pantry, the hamper) smell as they should, free of foreign odors.
f. Your humans are where they should be at that time of day, and that they have not changed your universe by rearranging furniture, leaving doors open unexpectedly, or otherwise creating whole new realms of

opportunity. (Ours once left a door open while they played an exciting new game called "Wallpapering the Den." We loved it!)

Tip: You can turn even this important task into a game for your humans simply by changing the way you go about it. We once spent a whole month refusing to step on the hall carpet. Humans are so easily entertained that they showed up almost every morning to admire our dexterity in putting all four feet in the three-inch space between the rug and the wall and to speculate endlessly on our various reasons for adopting this practice. These kindnesses cost you practically nothing and provide them with hours of fun, so why not give them a thrill?

See also: *"Keep Your Sunny Side Up"*
            Mysteries
            Placeology
            Televisions, Washing Machines,
                and Windows

32. Moon, how high the?

If you've read and applied everything in this book, you probably won't need this section. Nevertheless, humans are perverse, and the day might come—we know it's unlikely, but we have to say it—the day might come when you don't get your way. If this happens—that is, if you get stuck with a collar; if you're thrown off the chair, bed, or kitchen counter; if they serve you the breakfast that they know you don't like—consider your options. There are always strategic "accidents," but you don't want to use this powerful weapon every day.

The cat's intermediate-range tactical weapon is the "moon." Make eye contact with the humans, make sure you've got their attention, and then turn suddenly, with your tail lifted upright, giving a clear view of what is called a "moon" (ironically named for what doesn't shine there). They'll get the picture, and you will be considered witty in cat and human circles alike.

It's always appropriate to use the moon if you hear the word no, even if you're not certain of the context.

See also: *"Accidents"*
            Collars
            Eye Contact
            Training

33. Mysteries: Creating for human entertainment

Humans love mysteries! Therefore, they'll pay extra attention to the smart cat who creates one for them. How do you do this? Here are some of our most successful efforts.

When absolutely *nothing* is wrong:

a. Raise your head, cock your ears, and stare pointedly at (1) the outside door, (2) a corner where nothing is happening, (3) any place out of your humans' line of vision, or (4) (especially effective when only one human is present) one of their ears.

b. Walk to a visible (empty) corner and scratch frantically at the edge of the carpet, muttering loudly.

c. Refuse (for some 36 hours) to sit in your favorite place.

d. Pace up and down in the middle of the

room, swishing your tail and complaining loudly, twice a day for a week.

e. Insist on lying in a (comfortable) position you've never tried before.

f. Limp (intermittently).

(Some cats opt for refusing a favorite treat or otherwise changing eating habits. We don't encourage these tactics. First, because they might seriously alarm your humans—leading to the vet—and, second, because eating is a sacred rite that should be left alone.)

34. Nests

"Making the bed" is one of the central human mysteries. The fact is that *they* don't know why they do it, and most men don't do it at all. Humans really don't want to make the bed. So as soon as they get up, make a nest in the crumpled sheets and blankets. You'll be doing them a favor by providing an excuse for not making the bed. If they seem intent on making it anyway, see "Snooze Gas."

Nests are among the best places to rest. People usually provide them: the wool coat or sweater left on the bed or chair, the dry bath towel left on the floor, neatly packed suitcases, large hats, used grocery bags (many of which are endowed with magical properties), and so on. In general, avoid synthetic fibers when natural ones are available.

See also: *Beds*
             Placeology
             Snooze Gas

35. Petting: Setting the rules

Petting is great, but only one human in three gets it right, and then only 60 percent of the time. These are frightening odds. Cats are often put upon by the uneducated human who pets without first letting us smell the petting hand: Obviously, you want to know where it's been. Other petting perils include:

- Humans who pet in the wrong place. "Wrong places" vary from cat to cat and from day to day. Some days people are allowed to rub our tummies, but on other days they can lose a hand doing the same thing. Some humans think this is unfair. Who cares?

- Humans who pet you longer than you want to be petted. This, again, varies from cat to cat and from day to day.

Please understand, we're not trying to frighten you. Cats need never put up with any undignified, prolonged, or unwanted petting. Simply roll and purr when the petting's good, and when you're done, bite the petter's hand. It saves time.

See also: *Biting*
              Evasion

36. Placeology: Every cat should know her place(s)

Both authors have earned degrees in Placeology, the art and science of where to be. The effective cat will find places to sit, think, rest, sleep, groom, and so on, that not only feel good but also look good. For example: A cat sitting neatly centered atop the clothes dryer is not only a warm cat, but also a time-honored icon of domestic bliss. The only thing that's better is if there are neatly folded sweaters on the dryer. We're getting sleepy just thinking about it.

Other great places:

- Windowsills in the sunshine. They feel great, but your presence also proclaims to all passersby, human or feline, that yours is a home of distinction. It pays to advertise.
- Large "in" boxes full of paper.

- Obviously, floor heat vents are made for cats. We have heard of humans suffering from hypothermia because a single cat had absorbed all the BTUs the furnace could produce. How unfortunate for the humans—but what a cat!

- Boxes and bags, especially those endowed with the magical power of augmenting snooze gas. Magic bags are hard to find, so once you find one, don't leave it unattended.

Otherwise, be creative, and don't overlook the obscure and out-of-the-way. We have a gas stove with a pilot light under the top. We're embarrassed to admit that it took us some weeks to locate this "place of places," but it proved to be the thesis subject for our Ph.D. in Placeology.

See also: *Beds*
             Hiding
             "Keep Your Sunny Side Up"
             Location
             Snooze Gas

37. Recovery After Errors (rarely needed)

It's rare, but occasionally a cat will make a mistake in the presence of a human. It's never happened to us, but we've heard of cats falling off beds, missing jumps (or jumping onto highly polished surfaces only to slide off the other end), and the like.

Remember that when you show the slightest lack of agility or grace, you're not just letting yourself down; you're letting down all of catkind. Hence it is essential that you recover from what the Parisians call *le screw-up* immediately, unequivocally, and with grace. Landing on your feet isn't enough. You must then start cleaning vigorously, sending the message "I didn't fall; I did that on purpose in order to get a better cleaning angle." If anyone laughs, stare them down, finish cleaning, and shoot the moon.

See also: *Cleaning*
              Eye Contact
              Moon

38. Rubber Bands: A warning

Don't eat rubber bands. It seems like such a good idea, and they taste great, but you'll always regret it later. An acquaintance of ours eats rubber bands and, as a result, often leaves the litter box with the feeling that he is being followed. Don't eat rubber bands.

39. Schedules: Developing yours; managing theirs

Your day will generally divide into three segments: (a) sleeping, (b) eating, and (c) everything else. We recommend the following sequence:

a. Wake up
b. Eat
c. Other duties as assigned.*
d. Nap
e. See (a) through (d)

This schedule is comfortable, productive, healthful, and eminently catly.

But beware. Appropriate schedules do not fall into your lap as a gift from your humans. You must earn them by carefully training your

---

* Unscheduled opportunities to eat and sleep always take priority over any "other duties" assigned.

humans and guarding against their natural
tendency to backslide on important matters,
such as dinnertime. Use all the training tools
at your disposal (vocal instruction, example,
"accidents," mooning, withholding affection,
and the like) and remember the three rules
of successful human training: Be firm, be fair
(to yourself), be consistent.

40. Scratching posts: What are they for?

We have heard an ugly rumor that the objects known as scratching posts—pieces of wood with garish synthetic carpet—are intended for us. There are some slurs against humanity that even cats cannot tolerate. Sure, some people are dumb, but could they be *that* dumb? Why *buy* more things to scratch? Haven't they done enough by providing sofas, draperies, bedspreads, and expensive rugs?

We don't know what scratching posts are for, but they're not for us. *Please*, in the name of decency, do nothing to deface these objets d'art. We think humans worship them.

41. Sleeping (Theirs): Best ways to terminate

Two rules govern sleeping in the cat/human household:

a. Cats sleep whenever and wherever cats wish.
b. Humans sleep whenever and wherever cats wish.

Yet, without proper supervision, humans show an alarming tendency to sleep at inappropriate times (such as when you're hungry, when you want to play, and so on). To meet your responsibility as keeper of the family schedule, you must quickly master these tested techniques for terminating human slumber. They fall into two categories.

When the Human Is Asleep on the Wrong Side of a Closed Door

Your only option is to sing, call, threaten,

scratch on the door, and shout continuously until the human gives up and opens the door.
HINT: Your "racket" must be ceaseless, no matter how long this exercise takes. If you live in a multicat household, work in shifts.

When You Can Reach the Sleeping Human

Here you have many more options.

a. Tap him gently on the foot, hand, shoulder, cheek, nose, or mouth.

b. If this fails, start batting his favorite items off the bedside table, announcing each swipe before you make it and building gradually from his pens to his glasses.

c. If this fails, blow, or yell, in his ear.

d. If this fails, chew his hair.

e. If this fails, lick his eyelids.

f. If even this fails, lie down on his face.

42. Snooze Gas

The limits of human intelligence are nowhere clearer than in their inability to deduce the existence of "snooze gas." People have obviously noticed that they suddenly feel sleepy when they encounter slumbering cats, but they have dismissed the phenomenon as a stimulus/response brought about by the sight of the feline snoozer. They couldn't be further from the truth, but please don't tell them: Snooze gas is one of our most useful tools.

"Snooze gas"—not to be confused with the broader spectrum gases emanating from dogs—is an odorless, invisible vapor released through the pores of a sleeping and/or purring cat. People often wake with a cat on top of them (if they're lucky), wondering how they slept so long without detecting the guest. The answer, naturally, is snooze gas. People who have had prolonged contact with host cats gradually develop the capacity to emit the gas themselves ("snooze gasification"), although they never know it.

Humans who live with multiple cats and sleep with those cats in the same room may find themselves in a "snooze gas loop." Here two or more cats (and/or cat-minded humans) keep each other knocked out indefinitely (except for the call of food). The humans thus affected miss meals, appointments, and the like, but, fortunately, there are no undesirable side effects for the snoozing cats.

The strategic advantages of snooze gas are obvious. For instance, if you live with a human who is annoying you by watching too much football, MTV, CNN, or other noisy claptrap, all you have to do is curl up on or near the offending human. Once the snooze gas puts the TV watcher to sleep, another human will come to turn off the TV. Similarly, snooze gas is useful for creating laps on demand, and for keeping them.

43. Telephone Manners

Cat telephone etiquette is simple: If the phone rings, and you are the only one home—or the one closest to the phone—answer it. Otherwise, the caller will get the answering machine, leading him or her to believe that your humans are vulgar rubes.

Simply bat the receiver off the hook. Don't speak first; if it's for you, the callers will identify themselves. If it's not for you, leave the phone off the hook so you won't be bothered again.

44. Televisions, Washing Machines, and Windows: Is there a difference?

The cat entertainment center includes these items made for humans but perhaps truly appreciated only by us: televisions, washing machines, and windows.

The differences among these three are largely trivial, but we'll explain them for your convenience:

- *Windows* have sunlight; the others do not.

- *Windows* are larger than (most) TVs.

- Some *washing machines* don't have windows. These don't belong in your home entertainment schedule.

- *Windows* have better resolution than televisions, but *televisions* have fewer squirrels.

- Some *windows* have the "screen" option,

which actually lets you smell the
entertainment.

- For the best combination of resolution and
  program variety, the *washing machine* beats
  the other two every time.

- *Washing machines* have a very limited
  broadcast schedule; *windows* are available
  about 12 hours per day; *televisions*, 24.
  (Learn to use the remote control.)

45. Threats: Making/ignoring

From time to time, your window programming will offer the added excitement of Other Feline Persons (OFPs) trespassing in your yard. These occasions call for all resident cats to combine forces in making *terrible* threats.

Impressive threatening involves both verbal and nonverbal skills. Begin by offering a persistent low growl, while glaring at your opponent and slowly swelling to approximately ten times your normal size. (Note: When threatening from a windowsill, avoid embarrassment by remaining acutely aware of your need for adequate space.)

At the peak of your growth, crescendo into the loudest, most piercing note you can sustain, interrupting it only for furious hisses and fearsome, reverberating growls.

If this procedure inexplicably prompts the opposing feline to return the threat, turn

your back, stretch elaborately, and wash.
(There is, after all, a sturdy screen between
you and the Invader.)

46. Toilet Paper, tricks with

Toilet paper is the ultimate cat toy. (In fact, "toy" is the origin of the word "toilet.") Get up on your hind legs and pull, bat, or otherwise unroll the paper for hours of aerobic fun. Or take the leading edge in your teeth and see how far you can run without tearing the paper. The record is 247 feet, but there was no carpet in that arena. With modifications, the same holds true of paper towels.

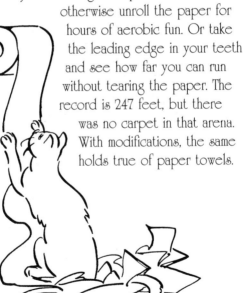

47. Training (your humans)

Many cats lack the patience to train humans properly, but we stand by the views we expressed in the Forepause: We persisted, and we've been glad we did. In our experience you can train humans successfully if you understand their limitations and focus on what they can, reasonably, be expected to learn.

You must always remember that humans *lose* capabilities as they age. Newborn humans, after all, can mew a little; small humans move fairly efficiently on all fours. As they grow, these skills desert them, as do their meager abilities to climb and leap. Adult humans are virtually inflexible, condemned to spend most of their waking hours precariously balanced on their hind legs. (Think about it!)

We've learned, however, that through consistent application of rewards, through

repetition, and through daily (sometimes
hourly) drilling, adult humans can be trained
to:

- Come when called.
- Bring heat to stoves and heaters.
- Create sunshine on windowsills.
- Feed; provide treats daily.
- Open (or close) doors.
- Play (at the least) ball, hide and seek, and
  "pencil, pencil, who's got the pencil."
- Provide entertainment (windows, TV, and
  so on), sometimes on demand.
- Provide frequent laps (generally on
  demand).
- Refrain from singing.
- Respect your "places."
- Respect your schedule.
- Sit, stand, lie down, and roll over,
  frequently on demand.

See also: *Attention*
             Basic Vocabulary (to ignore)
             Eye Contact

48. Treats

Like cat toys, treats are something humans think they understand. You probably already know how wrong they are.

Still, few cats wish to refuse an offered treat outright. First, because we're too gracious, and second, because it sends the

wrong message. Your objective, however, is to get the treats you really want. Try this:

When You Don't Want What's Offered

- Accept the offered treat with apparent delight, then bury it under the nearest available rug as soon as politeness permits. Meanwhile, lavish gratitude and affection on the donor.

When a Real Treat Appears

- Turn on the charm
- If that doesn't work, and you're in a multicat household, stage a distraction ploy and steal it.
- If *that* doesn't work, apply cunning and speed, and steal it anyway.

See also: *Blame*
              Cute, Being

49. Vets: Do we hate them?

Yes.

See also: *Biting*
           Evasion
           Hiding
           Threats

50. The Last Word

. . . like the first, is "love."

Love is knowing the *worst* about your humans (You've watched him sleep, haven't you? You've seen her grumpy and without her makeup) and still choosing to be with them every day.

Dead mice notwithstanding, love is truly the most special gift you can give.

How you tell your humans you love them (with a nose-to-nose kiss, a touch on the face when they're blue, a quiet word of encouragement, a special athletic event, a warm cuddle, or something unique and original) is, of course, up to you.

If you're lucky—and if you've mastered these rules, you're sure to be—they'll love you right back. Appreciate it; lives are short.

Grade 2.D ASH